# Just the Facts
# Genocide
## Sean Sheehan

Heinemann
LIBRARY

**www.heinemann.co.uk/library**
Visit our website to find out more information about **Heinemann Library** books.

To order:
☎ Phone 44 (0) 1865 888066
📄 Send a fax to 44 (0) 1865 314091
💻 Visit the Heinemann Bookshop at www.heinemann.co.uk/library to browse our catalogue and order online.

**Produced by Monkey Puzzle Media Ltd**
Gissing's Farm, Fressingfield, Suffolk IP21 5SH, UK

First published in Great Britain by Heinemann Library, Halley Court, Jordan Hill, Oxford OX2 8EJ, part of Harcourt Education.
Heinemann is a registered trademark of Harcourt Education Ltd.

Editorial: Daniel Rogers, Sarah Eason and Louise Galpine
Design: Mayer Media Ltd
Picture Research: Lynda Lines and Frances Bailey
Consultant: Ian Derbyshire
Production: Camilla Smith

Originated by Ambassador Litho Ltd
Printed and bound in Hong Kong, China by South China Printing Company

ISBN 0 431 16179 8
09 08 07 06 05
10 9 8 7 6 5 4 3 2 1

**British Library Cataloguing in Publication Data**
Sheehan, Sean
Genocide
304.6'63
A full catalogue record for this book is available from the British Library.

**Acknowledgements**
The publishers would like to thank the following for permission to reproduce photographs:
AKG-Images pp. **4 bottom, 7, 17 top right, 26, 31, 42–43**; Alamy p. **19** (David Hoffman); Corbis pp. **8** (Hulton-Deutsch Collection), **10** (Peter Turnley), **13** (Bettmann), **22** (Bettmann), **25** (Bettmann), **32** (Jacques Langevin/Sygma), **34** (Sygma), **35** (Hulton-Deutsch Collection), **37** (Bettmann), **40–41** (Sygma); Hulton Archive p. **27**; Mary Evans Picture Library p. **23** (Explorer/ Lenars); PA Photos/EPA pp. **11, 33, 44**; Reuters pp. **4 top** (Rafiqur Rahman), **20** (Damir Sagolj), **38** (François Lenoir), **46** (Nikola Solic), **49** (Damir Sagolj); Rex Features pp. **9** (Ron Cardy), **21** (SIPA), **28** (Roger Viollet); Still Pictures pp. **14–15** (Spyros Katsouris/UNEP), **16–17** (Jorgen Schytte); Topham Picturepoint p. **29 top** (Photonews).

Cover photograph reproduced with permission of Reuters (Danilo Krstanovic).

Every effort has been made to contact copyright holders of any material reproduced in this book. Any omissions will be rectified in subsequent printings if notice is given to the publishers.

Any words appearing in the text in bold, **like this**, are explained in the Glossary.

# Contents

# What is genocide?

**Genocide** is the carrying out of an intention to destroy a particular group of people. This is done either directly, through murder on a large scale, or indirectly by creating conditions that will lead to the group's destruction. In all cases of genocide, the victims belong to a group that is deliberately singled out and picked on. The intention is to kill members of that group, and the process of killing is carried out in a very organized way. In most cases, genocide is carried out by a government or with the permission of a government; especially when powerful or ruthless leaders are in charge.

## The victims of genocide

The victims of genocide are deliberately picked on because they belong to a particular group. It is often a mix of racial, **political**, economic and cultural factors that leads to a group becoming the victim of genocide.

English settlers, with superior weapons, fighting the original inhabitants of Australia, the Aboriginal people, in around 1840.

There are always political associations with acts of genocide. Political means to do with relations of power in society, and the ways in which one group or class of people maintains its power and influence over another group of people. Economic factors also often play a part in genocide. Many acts of genocide involve taking land and property from the victims.

The victims of a genocide are a group of civilians who are generally unarmed.

The same group can be both responsible for genocide and, in another time and place, the victims of genocide. Muslim groups, such as that seen protesting here in 1999 against the persecution of Muslims in Kosovo, were responsible in 1917 for the Armenian genocide in Turkey.

Genocide usually occurs in a war situation. This is not the same as the **mass killing** of unarmed civilians that can happen in a war. Genocide means killing a group of civilians with the intention of destroying their identity. A group's identity is a matter of **culture**, meaning that it relates to the customs and beliefs of that group. Part of this culture is how the group defines itself as different from other groups.

Sometimes genocide is not just a matter of killing. For a long time after the British arrived in Australia in 1788, large numbers of Aboriginal people (the people already living there) were killed, but the genocide also involved forcibly removing children from their families and placing them in special homes or the homes of white foster parents. There, the children lost knowledge of their own culture and had to learn a new one.

More usually, though, genocide is about killing. Around six million Jews were murdered in Europe as a result of the **Nazi** party gaining power in Germany in 1933. It was because of what the Nazis did that the word genocide came into existence. Acts of genocide, however, were carried out before the Nazis, and such acts continue to be carried out.

# Genocide before the Nazis

The word **genocide** is recent – it was first used in 1944 – but the crime is an ancient one. In the legends and history of **Assyria**, ancient Greece and Rome, there are many accounts of warfare that tell of the slaughter of entire communities and the destruction of their **culture**. When the non-Greek city of Troy was captured and burnt to the ground in about 1260 BCE, the male population was killed and the women and children were carried off as slaves by the Greek warriors. In 146 BCE, the inhabitants of Carthage in North Africa – one of the greatest cities in ancient times – were treated in the same way by the Romans, who also ploughed salt into their land to prevent crops ever being grown there again.

The religious wars known as the **Crusades** (1096–1272), when Christian armies invaded the **Middle East**, involved large-scale massacres not only of Muslims but also Jews. Later, in 16th-century Europe, religious conflicts between Catholics and Protestants led to massacres of groups singled out because of their religion. The slaughter of thousands of Huguenot Protestants, for example, was carried out on 23–24 August 1572 in Paris, on the orders of the French king Charles IX – an event known as the St Bartholomew's Day Massacre.

## The Armenian genocide

By the early 20th century, more advanced technology and forms of communication made it possible for governments to organize genocide in a more systematic way. The genocide of Armenians in Turkey in 1915–16, which cost the lives of over one million

Several thousand Huguenot Protestants were targeted and killed in Paris on 23–24 August 1572.

people, is an example of this. Armenians were accused of disloyalty to the Turkish **nation** at a time when the country was at war. They were not Muslims and had their own culture and language, making it easy to single them out and treat them as a **scapegoat**.

Armenian men, who had earlier been made to join the Turkish army, were forced to disarm. Educated Armenians, who might have been able to organize protest and resistance, were arrested, tortured and killed. Armenian men still at liberty were then collected together in towns and villages, marched away from public view and massacred. Women and children were forced to march out of the country and into the desert of neighbouring Syria where they were left to die. On these journeys, the police who were guarding the Armenians organized murderous attacks on them using local villagers and prisoners released from jail for this purpose.

# The Holocaust

The attempt to kill all the Jews in Europe, known as the **Holocaust**, has its origin in the rise to power of Hitler and his **Nazi** party in Germany in 1933. In the years that followed, a series of steps were taken that can be seen as preparing the ground for the Holocaust. Jewish people were first dismissed from government jobs, then from most jobs that earned a decent rate of pay. Laws were passed forcing Jews to sell any businesses they owned, then laws made it illegal for non-Jewish Germans to marry Jews. Another law forced Jews to wear a distinctive yellow star in public. Eventually Jews were collected together and forced to live in restricted areas, called **ghettoes**, where thousands were left to die. By January 1942, at a meeting in Wannsee outside Berlin, top-ranking Nazis decided on what they called 'the final solution', the organized killing of every Jew in Europe.

There are aspects of the Holocaust that make it a very special, unique event. It happened during **World War II** but even when the Nazis knew they were losing the war they continued to devote valuable resources to the task of organizing the **genocide**. Nazis and their supporters worked out in careful detail how they could most efficiently murder Jews. It was carried out like a business.

Organized by the Nazis, demonstrators in Berlin, Germany, in the 1930s, distribute **anti-Semitic** pamphlets to passers-by.

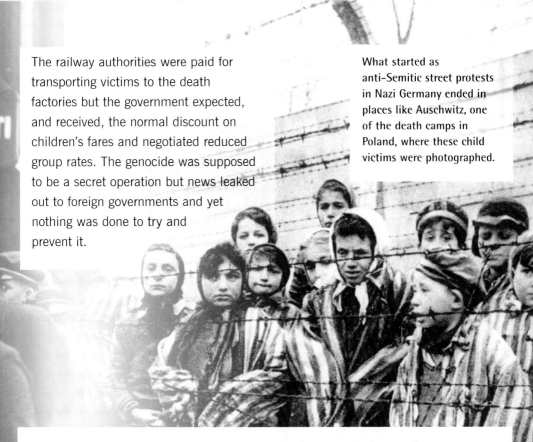

The railway authorities were paid for transporting victims to the death factories but the government expected, and received, the normal discount on children's fares and negotiated reduced group rates. The genocide was supposed to be a secret operation but news leaked out to foreign governments and yet nothing was done to try and prevent it.

What started as anti-Semitic street protests in Nazi Germany ended in places like Auschwitz, one of the death camps in Poland, where these child victims were photographed.

# Case study  The final solution

Between 1942 and 1945, the Nazis killed around 4 million Jews in death factories called **concentration camps**, most of which were in Poland, including Auschwitz, where over 1 million were killed. A further 2 million were killed in the ghettoes or by shooting squads. At the concentration camps, prisoners were gassed in specially constructed gas chambers designed to look like showers. Their dead bodies were then burnt in huge ovens. Other killing methods included piping the poisonous exhaust fumes of vans back into the vehicles in which victims were locked, as well as shooting, starving or working them to death, and carrying out lethal medical experiments on them.

Jews were not the only targets of Nazi genocide. Other victims – totalling around 5 million – included **communists**, so-called 'inferior' races such as Russians and Poles, gypsies, homosexuals and the mentally ill.

# Recent holocausts

**Genocide** did not come to an end with the defeat of **Nazi** Germany in 1945. Recent decades have witnessed more acts of genocide in different parts of the world.

## Indonesia

A struggle for **political** power in Indonesia led, in 1965, to the Indonesian army and their supporters killing **communists** all over the country. Around half a million people were murdered. Ten years later, the army conducted another genocide, this time against the people of neighbouring East Timor. Indonesia wanted control of East Timor and, although there was no plan to kill every East Timorese, more than 200,000 died, women were **sterilized** against their will and a mass immigration of Indonesians into East Timor was encouraged. The immigrants were given all the best jobs as part of a policy to destroy the Timorese sense of independence and identity. This genocide was in progress until 1999, when the **United Nations** helped bring it to an end. East Timor is now independent.

## Cambodia and Rwanda

The genocide that took place in Cambodia between 1975 and 1979 was also political in its nature. After a **civil war** in the country, a Communist party called Khmer Rouge and led by Pol Pot took power and drove everyone out of the cities and closed schools and factories. There was a plan to build a new society in the countryside and anyone who might not help was killed. Professional people such as teachers and doctors, targeted as enemies because of their economic and social background, were executed in large numbers. Work conditions were extremely harsh and there were regular executions. In total, at least one and a half million people died as a result of starvation and executions.

Hutus, forming a military unit from the civilian population, practise marching with mock wooden rifles on a main road in Rwanda in 1994.

A recent genocide took place in Rwanda in central Africa and in the course of just a few months hundreds of thousands of people were killed. Every Tutsi, the minority **ethnic group** in the country, was targeted for murder by the majority Hutu group. At one time, the Tutsis had enjoyed political control but when the country became independent in 1962 the Hutus took power. By 1990, the Hutu government was under pressure to share some of its power with Tutsis but its reluctance to do so lead to fighting and difficult times for everyone. High-ranking Hutus began arming their people and plans were made for the killing of not only all Tutsis but also any moderate Hutus who were prepared to share power. Special troops were trained to kill up to 1000 people every twenty minutes and the genocide, which began in April 1994, resulted in the deaths of around 500,000 people in just a hundred days.

In East Timor in 1999, villagers searching for their missing relatives unearth a shallow grave likely to contain the remains of a genocide victim. The grave was located behind a former military camp of the Indonesians.

11

# Seeking explanations

## Historical explanations

Seeking an explanation for **genocide** involves looking at the facts of different acts of genocide and seeing what they have in common. Most genocides have a **political** cause in the sense that one class of people, usually in control of a country's government, seeks to keep power by killing another group. An example of this took place in 1971 when the Bengali people of East Pakistan were struggling to form the new **nation** of Bangladesh. The Pakistani government wanted to prevent this from happening and set out to terrorize the Bengali population. In an organized way, males were killed and women were raped. One and a half million people died.

Often, though, the political nature of genocide is bound up with other, different, causes. The Jews in Germany were not threatening to weaken **Nazi** power, nor had they done anything in particular to anger the Nazi government. In order to understand the causes of such different genocides it is necessary to look at what happened in the past. The history of different groups in a society, and the past relations between those committing genocide and the group making up the victims provides important information. This is what is meant by an **historical approach** to the causes of genocide.

## Psychological explanations

Historical facts are essential for understanding why a government comes to plan genocide. However, a government is made up of individual people and it can be difficult to understand why individuals choose such an extreme and murderous way of dealing with a situation. It is equally difficult to understand why ordinary people carry out genocide and why they murder, not one person but tens and hundreds of them. The kind of explanation that would help explain this is what is meant by a **psychological approach** (psychological meaning to do with the mind or the mental state of people). Understanding genocide, and trying to prevent it in the future, needs a historical and a psychological approach. The genocide in Cambodia, for example, is best understood in both historical and psychological terms.

East Pakistanis flee to India from the threat of genocide at the hands of the Pakistani authorities in December 1971.

# Traumatic times

Many acts of **genocide** occur when a country is in trauma, suffering the physical and psychological shocks of a war. At such times, ordinary life becomes extremely stressful and people feel threatened and insecure. The human need for a sense of belonging to a community may, in **traumatic** situations, lead people to join extreme groups and adopt their ideas. In some cases, this may lead to genocide. Cambodia is one example of this.

## Cambodia

Cambodia had, for centuries, been a peaceful, Buddhist society where most people lived in villages, growing rice and not harming each other. Everything changed when a war developed in neighbouring Vietnam between US and North Vietnamese forces. Between 1969 and 1973, the USA began bombing Cambodia, in order to target routes that Vietnamese forces were suspected of using to transport supplies. Thousands of bombing raids destroyed villages, killing people and driving refugees into the capital city. At its most intense, in 1973, 3500 tonnes of bombs were being dropped a day, and the Cambodian government was overthrown in a US-backed invasion of the country. The Khmer Rouge party

Cambodia remembers the genocide that took place in the country under the rule of the Khmer Rouge. This display case holds the skulls and bones of prisoners killed by the regime.

arose from the ashes of rural Cambodia and peasants, whose way of life had been turned upside down, were encouraged to join it. After two years of fighting, the Khmer Rouge, which adopted an extreme way of dealing with the country's plight, took over the government. Genocide resulted as the Khmer Rouge, under their leader Pol Pot, set about killing anyone who was seen as an enemy of the pure, new society they wanted to create.

**"Their minds just froze up and they would wander around mute [unable to speak] for three or four days. Terrified and half-crazy, the people were ready to believe what they were told... That was what made it so easy for the Khmer Rouge to win the people over... It was because of their dissatisfaction with the bombing that they kept on cooperating with the Khmer Rouge, joining up with the Khmer Rouge, sending their children off to go with them."**

Chhit Do., a Khmer Rouge Cambodian, describing how peasants were affected by the bombing and how this helped bring the Khmer Rouge to power. From *The Pol Pot Regime*, Ben Kiernan.

# Accusing others

Guatemalans of Mayan descent, distinguished by their traditional forms of dress, shopping at a street market in Guatemala.

Most countries that experience **traumatic** times do not turn to **genocide** so there must also be other factors that lead to killing an entire group of people. One important factor is a history of 'us' and 'them' within the country where genocide takes place. The victims of genocide belong to a group that is often seen to deserve its suffering *because* of what the group is accused of having done, or because of who they are. Very often, they are accused of something simply because of who they are. Blaming other people for one's problems and identifying a **scapegoat** is not unusual. It offers a false understanding of why something unpleasant is happening and provides psychological comfort.

## Nazi Germany

The Jews were the scapegoats for **Nazis** in Germany, and the Nazis were feeding off a long history of **anti-Semitism** (prejudice against Jews) in Europe. Jews had been persecuted for centuries and Christianity reinforced this prejudice by treating them as unbelievers and the killers of Christ. Jews looked different, because of their customs, their different ways of dressing and religious practices. This made it easy to see them as just a group rather than as individuals who happened to belong to a particular group.

This medieval woodcut, depicting Jews accused of **heresy** being burned, is evidence of the long tradition of anti-Semitism in Europe.

# Guatemala and Turkey

Something similar can be seen again in the treatment of the Guatemalan people who became the victims of genocide in their own country. The victims were the descendants of the original Maya people who lived in Guatemala before the Spanish conquered the country in the 16th century. Making up more than half the population, they are the poorest and most downtrodden group in the country. The ruling class of the country, descendants of intermarriage with the Spanish, has always regarded these people as inferior. When a struggle for more equal rights began in 1960, the Guatemalans of Mayan descent were all accused of being **communists** trying to bring down the government. The government, unwilling to accept demands for equal rights, blamed them for the **political** unrest. Over the next 36 years, more than 200,000 people were killed as the army singled them out for persecution.

In the genocide in Turkey in 1915–16, there was also a history of devaluing the Armenian people. There had been episodes of **mass killing** in the past and, as we have seen, the Armenians became a scapegoat for Turkey's problems.

# Nationalism

**Nationalism** is a strong attachment to one's country, and nationalists regard their own **nation** very highly. This is usually expressed in harmless ways, such as supporting a country's soccer team, but it can also find expression in the belief that one country is superior to another. At its most extreme, nationalism becomes a form of racism. A nationalist, thinking that their nation or their race is superior, can regard people seen as belonging to a different nation or race as inferior. This kind of 'us'-and-'them' attitude makes it easier for one group to accuse another group of having done something for which they deserve to be punished.

> **"Khmer bodies with Vietnamese minds."**
>
> A reason given by the Khmer Rouge for killing not just Cambodians of Vietnamese descent but Khmer people as well. From *The Pol Pot Regime*, Ben Kiernan.

The **Nazis** encouraged German nationalism and many highly educated people were attracted to the idea. Nazis encouraged belief in the idea of a pure German race that was in danger of being 'polluted' by other races that they labelled as inferior. Such extreme nationalism made it easier to think of Jews as people who deserved to be set apart and sent off to special camps.

In Rwanda, Hutus were encouraged to think that the Tutsis were not natural Rwandans. They were labelled as invaders, immigrants of an inferior kind who could not be trusted. In Turkey, in the years leading up to the Armenian **genocide**, there was a powerful party of nationalists called the Young Turks. They wanted to restore the glory of a Turkish Muslim identity that had existed in the recent past. They encouraged a nationalist sense of identity that did not include Armenians. Most of the leaders who organized the genocide belonged to the Young Turks.

In a very different part of the world, very similar ideas shaped the attitudes and behaviour of the Khmer Rouge party that took control of Cambodia in 1975. The party had a strong sense of national identity and Khmer people were seen as the 'pure' Cambodians and other non-Khmer groups of citizens, such as people of Vietnamese descent, were regarded as inferior immigrants who deserved to be expelled or killed. When the Khmer Rouge murdered their own people, they justified their actions by accusing the victims of thinking like non-Khmers.

The National Front associate their nationalism with a dislike of foreigners and call for an end to immigration to the UK.

# Case study:
# Serb nationalism

Serbia and Bosnia, along with four other states, were once part of Yugoslavia, a country that by 1990 was breaking up. In March 1992, Bosnia voted to become an independent state and was recognized as such by the European Union and the USA. Serbia, however, would not accept this and began arming the Serbs living in Bosnia, who made up about one-third of Bosnia's population. Serbia was led by Slobodan Milosevic, an extreme **nationalist** who wanted to create a 'Greater Serbia'.

Milosevic became powerful because he was able to appeal to Serbian nationalists in Bosnia as well as Serbia. By claiming that the Serbs were the 'natural' people of Yugoslavia, he devalued other **ethnic groups** and especially the Muslims of Bosnia. Milosevic gave Serbs an excuse for taking land that belonged to Muslims but this, of course, created bitterness and divisions between people who had once lived peacefully alongside one another.

Milosevic and his nationalist supporters, notably Radovan Karadzic, the leader of Serbs living in Bosnia, set about a highly organized persecution of the Muslims, using methods that have become familiar from other acts of **genocide** around the world. Civilians were rounded up before being tortured and murdered in large numbers, and women were raped because they were Muslims. Special camps were built where Muslim men were concentrated together and kept in extremely harsh conditions. Much of what happened was carried out by Serb civilians, not regular army soldiers. The aim was to create, through '**ethnic cleansing**', areas which contained only Serbs. The **civil war** in Bosnia, between Muslims, Serbs and Croats, claimed over 200,000 lives between 1992 and 1995.

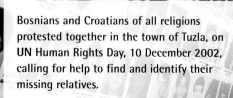

Bosnians and Croatians of all religions protested together in the town of Tuzla, on UN Human Rights Day, 10 December 2002, calling for help to find and identify their missing relatives.

# 'I no longer know you'

A Bosnian Serb, rounding up Muslims in a town in Bosnia, knocked on the door of a Muslim family. The woman who opened the door realized what was happening but she also recognized the face of the young man because he was her neighbour: 'Visovic, you know me, you know my husband... How can you do this to me?' Visovic replied: 'That time is over. I no longer know you'. The woman was forced by Visovic to crawl along the street, being continually kicked by her neighbour.

From *Becoming Evil*, James Waller.

Arkan (left) was a Serb commander in the Balkan conflict, and was accused of carrying out **atrocities**. He was assassinated in 2000.

# Colonialism and imperialism

A **colony** is formed when a group of people base themselves in another country and settle down and rule it. When this is organized on a large scale, usually by a government or a powerful group, it is called **colonialism**. The cause of colonialism is economic, to do with making money, and the profits that are made in a colony are often sent back to the colonizing country.

## The Congo

In the late 19th century, in what is now called the Democratic Republic of Congo, there was a **genocide** that took place as a direct result of colonialism. It happened because one king wanted to have his own colony. King Leopold II of Belgium saw Britain, France and Germany creating colonies in Africa and elsewhere and he wanted one for himself. In 1885, he claimed the Congo for himself and set about making himself enormously rich by selling ivory and rubber that came from the Congo. Thousands of

King Leopold II of Belgium defeated an Anglo-Portuguese attempt to conquer the Congo in Central Africa, gained recognition by the USA and was accepted as the ruler of the Congo Free State, an area 80 times the size of Belgium.

people were murdered and many thousands more died of starvation when villages were destroyed and the men forced to work as slaves producing rubber. There was never an intention to kill everyone, because people were needed to work, yet during the Leopold period, the population dropped by around ten million people. Many died of disease – largely as a result of being continually overworked in unhealthy conditions and being underfed – but the colonial power was not bothered by this.

Spanish **imperialism** in the 16th century led to acts of slaughter in Central America, such as the massacre of Aztecs depicted here. Today such acts would be labelled genocide.

## Guatemala

The economic factor is often not openly admitted in acts of colonialism, and religious or ethnic matters disguise what is really going on. In Guatemala, for example, the ethnic differences within the country today are bound up with the fact that a tiny proportion of the population, belonging to one **ethnic group**, own most of the farming land. The fighting that led to the genocide of the Guatemalans of Mayan descent was a struggle over the ownership of land. The land came to be unequally divided in the first place because Spain colonized the country in the early 16th century and gained control of the best farming land. The genocide that took place between 1960 and 1996 was a legacy of Guatemala's colonial history.

# Imperialism and genocide

Creating colonies is often part of a country's ambition to extend its control and influence. A powerful state may want to bring other countries under its authority and create an **empire**. This is called imperialism, and in some cases it helps to explain why genocide takes place.

## The Herero

German imperialism led to a number of colonies being created in Africa and in 1885 Hereroland, now part of Namibia, became one of them. The Herero people kept cattle on their land but the colonists wanted the land for themselves and, over a number of years, took it away from the Herero. By 1904, angry at having lost so much of their land, the Herero rose in rebellion. Soldiers under General von Trotha were sent in by the German government to crush the rebellion and von Trotha, having put down the rebellion, decided that the Herero should all be killed.

The Herero, cornered in a part of their land close to a desert, were driven into the desert and left to die of thirst. The soldiers were ordered to kill any Herero who attempted to return: 'Every Herero, whether found with or without a rifle, with or without cattle, shall be shot... No male prisoners will be taken', read von Trotha's written order. Within two years, around 60,000 Hereros were killed and those who survived became slave workers for the German colonists.

## Nanking and Manila

In the 1930s, Japanese imperialism led to the invasion of China. The imperialist ambitions of Japan were strongly based on ideas of racial superiority over other Asian peoples, including the Chinese. When Nanking (now called Nanjing), then the capital of China, was captured in December 1937 there followed a genocidal massacre of the city's inhabitants that became known as 'the rape of Nanking'. An estimated 260,000 civilians died. In 1945, during **World War II**, something similar happened in Manila, the capital of the Philippines, where it is estimated 100,000 civilians were killed by the Japanese.

**"**Tens of thousands of young men were rounded up and herded to the outer areas of the city, where they were mowed down by machine guns, used for **bayonet** practice, or soaked with gasoline and burned alive. For months the streets of the city were heaped with corpses and reeked with the stench of rotting human flesh.**"**

From *The Rape of Nanking: The Forgotten Holocaust of World War II*, Iris Chang.

Japanese forces marching through the gates of the city of Nanking in 1937. The Chinese citizens of Nanking became victims of Japanese genocide.

# The power of the state

What is meant by the power of the state is the way in which a government can possess a great amount of authority and control over its citizens. In the case of an **imperialist** country, this power may affect the lives of people belonging to other **nations**. **Genocide** is usually related to the power of the state, and it is usually a government that provides the authority and the means for people to carry out genocide. When a government is led by a particularly powerful and ruthless leader, as the **USSR** was led by Stalin, the result can be genocide.

## Stalin

Joseph Stalin became the most important **political** leader of the USSR in the early 1920s. He created an **empire**, ruled by **communist** Russia, and he was determined to keep this power.

The USSR was made up of different nationalities and Stalin and his government were afraid that some of these might threaten their overall authority and control. The land-owning peasants of the Ukraine, one of the 15 republics making up the USSR, were seen as a particular threat because of their sense of independence and in 1932–33 they became the victims of genocide. The Ukrainians were ordered to produce an impossibly high quantity of grain, their existing grain stores were taken from them by force, and food was prevented from reaching them from outside. In all, somewhere between four and six million Ukrainians died.

What happened to the Ukrainians was not an isolated event under Stalin's government. Any group of people who were seen as a threat to the power of the state was targeted. Special prison camps were built for 'enemies of the state' and countless thousands of others were collected together and **deported** to remote parts of the USSR, like Siberia, where living conditions were very harsh.

Joseph Stalin (1879–1953), the son of a shoemaker, rose to become the leader of the USSR in 1922. Ruling until his death, his ruthless policies led to genocide.

People were packed into railway wagons for the long journey, without food or heating, and many died on the way.

Stalin's political genocide continued during the 1930s and, after **World War II**, it happened again. Whole nations, like the Chechens and the Tartars, were accused of having sided with Nazi Germany. Mass deportations took place once again and huge numbers of people died.

Homeless peasants gather near Kiev, Ukraine, then part of the USSR, where they became the victims of a forced famine under Stalin.

# The trouble with facts

The trouble with facts is that not everyone accepts them, especially when the facts point to uncomfortable truths. Governments are not inclined to plead guilty to a crime as serious as **genocide**. The government of Germany is unusual in that it fully accepts what happened under **Nazi** rule. It has paid large amounts of compensation to Jewish organizations representing **Holocaust** survivors and their families and built Holocaust museums and memorials. Young Germans read about their country's past in school history books. The same is not true in the case of the Armenian genocide.

## Denying genocide

The Turkish government does not accept that Armenians were the victims of genocide. It does not deny that many Armenians died but claims that the total number of victims was a lot less. It also argues that the mass **deportations** were necessary because Armenians were disloyal, supporting Turkey's enemies in World War I. Outside of Turkey, the Armenian genocide is accepted as a fact by historians around the world. The Turkish government has been successful in denying the genocide only because,

Victims of the genocide of Armenians that took place in Turkey during World War I.

David Irving at home in London in 2000 at the time of the trial at the Old Bailey. He lost his case, which rested on the false claim that Hitler was not responsible for the Holocaust.

it is said, countries like the USA and Britain want to maintain friendly relations with Turkey.

Hardly anyone denies the genocide of Jews because there is so much evidence of what happened, including witnesses who were there in the death factories. In 2000, however, historian David Irving became briefly famous for claiming there had never been any organized destruction of Jews across Europe. He took legal action against the publisher and author of a book that had accused him of denying the genocide. His case was examined in a court of law and failed.

Another way in which people deny genocide is by finding innocent-sounding ways of describing what they do. The organized killing that took place in Bosnia was called '**ethnic cleansing**', which makes it sound hygienic and harmless. The Hutus in Rwanda described what they were doing as 'bush clearing'.

# What counts as genocide?

In the cases looked at so far, there is little serious argument that what happened was **genocide**. There are other cases, with similarities to some of these genocides, where there is disagreement about the dividing line between genocide and mass killing.

## Native Americans

The history of the Native Americans is one example of this. On the one hand, it was never the policy of the US government deliberately to **exterminate** the Native Americans. However, the government was always ready to kill them when it was felt to be necessary. There were plenty of large-scale massacres, openly reported in local newspapers, and no effort was made to stop or punish the killers. Earlier in the history of North America, British forces had acted in a similar way and, for example, given the Native Americans blankets infected with diseases in order to kill them.

## Bombing civilians

In **World War II**, the bombing of each other's cities by Germany and Britain gradually developed into a deliberate policy on Britain's part to kill civilians as a way of weakening the **morale** of the enemy. This policy led to an attack on Hamburg in 1943 that killed around 45,000 people, and an attack on Dresden in 1945 that killed about 70,000. Soon after Dresden, US planes bombed Tokyo and around 80,000 civilians died. The war came to an end when US planes dropped two atomic bombs on the cities of Hiroshima and Nagasaki and over 200,000 civilians were killed.

This killing of Germans and Japanese was a means to an end, that of winning the war. The killing was not an end in itself and cannot be considered genocide in the way that the **Nazi** killing of Jews can. Nevertheless, the British and US bombing did involve the deliberate mass killing of unarmed civilians on the grounds of their nationality. Although there was no deliberate intention to commit genocide, what took place was very similar to what happens when an act of genocide is committed.

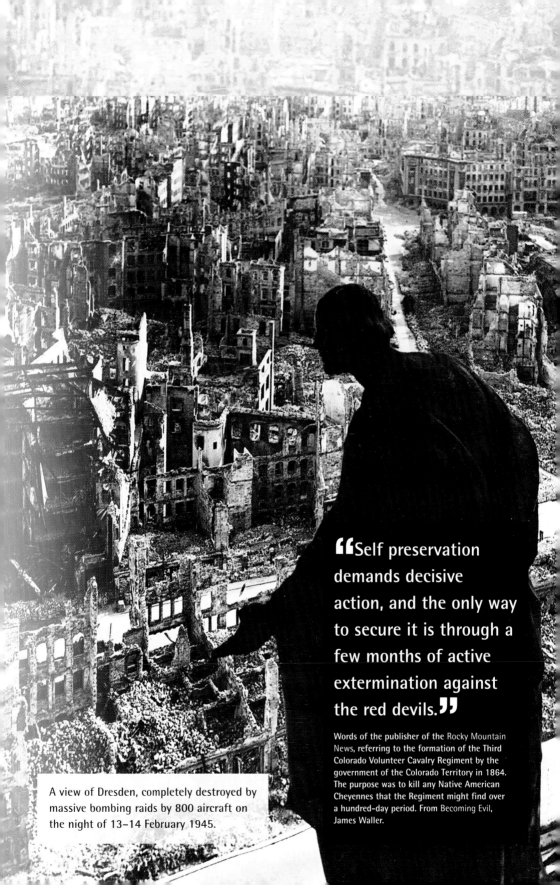

“Self preservation demands decisive action, and the only way to secure it is through a few months of active extermination against the red devils.”

Words of the publisher of the Rocky Mountain News, referring to the formation of the Third Colorado Volunteer Cavalry Regiment by the government of the Colorado Territory in 1864. The purpose was to kill any Native American Cheyennes that the Regiment might find over a hundred-day period. From Becoming Evil, James Waller.

A view of Dresden, completely destroyed by massive bombing raids by 800 aircraft on the night of 13–14 February 1945.

# Who is to blame?

In one sense, it is easy to know who is to blame for **genocide** because there are always the individual people who physically commit the various acts of murder that make up genocide. Arguments about this will involve lawyers in a courtroom presenting evidence for the guilt or innocence of an accused individual. When people and organizations, like a government or the **mass media** are involved in genocide – even though they did not physically kill anyone – there are different kinds of argument.

## Selling weapons

It has been argued, for example, that the ethnic divisions that led to genocide in Rwanda would have been easier to heal, and would not have led to genocide, were it not for the involvement of other countries. France wanted to maintain its influence in central Africa and kept on friendly terms with the Rwandan government. In the early 1990s, France secretly supplied Rwanda with money, weapons and military training; Egypt also sold the Rwandan government a large amount of weapons. Rwanda, a very small country, became the third largest importer of weapons in Africa and the weapons contributed to the very high numbers of victims in the genocide and to the speed of the killing. Governments that sell weapons, or governments that allow weapons to be sold in this way, argue that they would not have done so had they known what they were going to be used for.

## The mass media

The mass media – television, newspapers and radio – may also be involved in genocide. This was the case in Serbia where newspapers encouraged the kind of ethnic hatred that led to genocide. In Rwanda, radio broadcasts were made actively calling on the Hutu population to go out and kill Tutsis.

Jean-Bosco Barayagwiza, a journalist accused of genocide, sits in the Appeals Court of the International Criminal Tribunal for Rwanda.

The mass media in the West – in the USA and Europe – have also been accused of indirectly allowing some genocides to develop, or to continue when they could have been stopped. It is said that television stations and newspapers do not cover foreign news properly because they think this will not attract readers or viewers. It is also argued that when they do cover genocidal conflicts in foreign countries, the mass media only show sensational bits of news and do not bother to explain the causes of the conflicts. This makes it more difficult for people to know what is happening and to try to influence the policies of their governments.

One of the many annual international arms exhibitions held around the world. This one in Pakistan in 2000 attracted government purchasers from more than 30 countries.

# Willing executioners?

As well as the individuals who actually commit acts of **genocide**, there are also people who stand by and allow such acts to take place. To what extent should such people be blamed for what happens? In extreme cases, is it possible that people not only allow genocide to take place but actually want it to take place?

A book about the genocide of Jews caused a great deal of argument when it was published a few years ago. Daniel Goldhagen, in his book *Hitler's Willing Executioners: Ordinary Germans and the Holocaust*, claimed that Jews were the victims of genocide because this is what ordinary Germans wanted. German people were willing executioners, driven by a deep-rooted prejudice against Jews. Most ordinary Germans, the book claims, wanted Jewish people to be **eliminated** from their society.

Nearly all historians think that Goldhagen was mistaken with some of his facts and his general idea. They point to the fact that it was not only Germans who carried out the genocide. In France, there was also deep prejudice against Jews and a willingness to **deport** them from their country. In the Channel Islands,

occupied by the **Nazis**, British policemen helped with the deportation of Jews who ended up being gassed in the death factories in Poland. In Eastern Europe, in countries like Latvia, Lithuania and Romania, hundreds of thousands of Jews were massacred without the killers being forced to do so by Germans. Such examples show that people of any nationality can think or act in ways that allow genocide to take place or even participate in genocide.

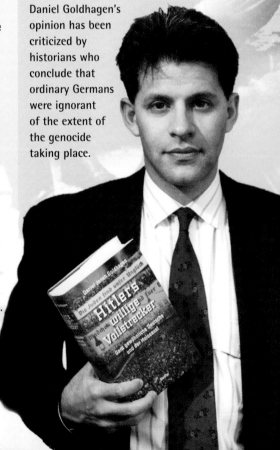

Daniel Goldhagen's opinion has been criticized by historians who conclude that ordinary Germans were ignorant of the extent of the genocide taking place.

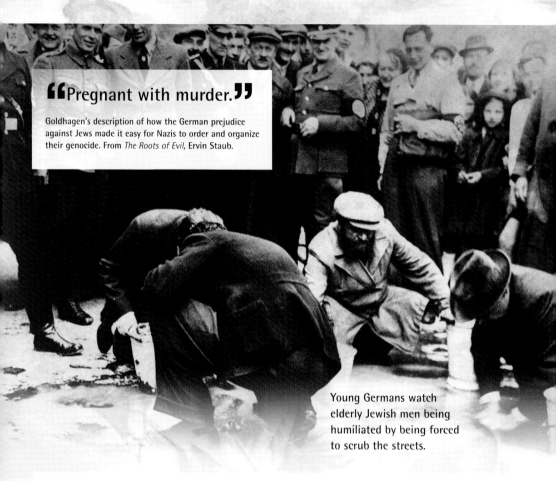

Young Germans watch elderly Jewish men being humiliated by being forced to scrub the streets.

It is also a fact that the Nazi party, which came to power in 1933, had the support of only 33 per cent of German voters. The majority of Germans did not vote for the Nazis. Once in power, though, the Nazis quickly began imprisoning people who dared to disagree with them and only then began making life more and more difficult for Jews.

Historians agree that there was a history of **anti-Semitism** across Europe. For example, in early 20th century Russia there were a succession of mob attacks, known as **pogroms**, on Jews. Without this history, Hitler and his party would not have been able to organize the Holocaust. Historians, however, reject the idea that most ordinary Germans wanted the Jews removed from their world and that they allowed genocide to occur because they wanted it to happen. Some historians accuse Goldhagen himself of displaying a racist attitude, because he accuses the German **nation** as a whole of having an anti-Semitic character.

# Is human nature to blame?

In 1960, a **Nazi** who played an important part in the **Holocaust** was arrested. The man, Adolf Eichmann, had organized the transport that brought Jews from all over Europe to the death factories. He knew the Jews were being murdered and when his trial was televised many people watched with fascination. They expected to see a psychopath, a man filled with murderous hate, but what they saw was a very normal-looking man. In court, he looked and behaved like an ordinary person. There was no medical evidence to suggest that Eichmann was mad or deeply disturbed in some psychological way. The fact is that **genocide** is not carried out by psychopaths but by people who seem ordinary, people with families, people who wear suits and have regular jobs.

Apart from humans it is rare for members of the animal kingdom to kill each other in this kind of way. This raises the question of whether there is something built into our human nature that makes us like this. One day, a group of scientists might claim they have discovered the 'genocide **gene**', something in our **biological** make-up that allows us to commit genocide.

There are facts that make it unlikely that genocide could ever be usefully explained in this kind of way. People are not computers and human nature is not a microchip that programs us to act in certain ways. Most people, most of the time, do not kill other people. The tendency to show kindness and affection towards other people is far more common than the tendency to want to kill. Examples of genocide show that it happens in some circumstances and not in others. It has to do with how groups and individuals relate to one another and how conflict is expressed. The history of how conflict between groups of people turns into genocide suggests that it has more to do with how some governments behave than with the idea that people are born with an instinct for **mass killing**.

**❝I sat at my desk and did my work.❞**

The words of Eichmann, on trial for helping to organize the murder of six million people. From *The Capture and Trial of Adolf Eichmann*, M Pearlman.

Karl Adolf Eichmann (1906–62), tracked down to Argentina by Israeli agents, was seized and brought to Jerusalem to stand trial for his part in organizing the Holocaust. He was executed there in 1962.

# Genocide and the law

Demonstrators outside a court in Belgium demanding that Israeli Prime Minister Ariel Sharon face charges for his role in the massacre of Palestinians.

**SHARON**

**ASSASSIN**

The word **genocide** was first used by a Polish legal expert, Raphael Lemkin. He saw the need for a new word to describe the deliberate act of picking on a particular group of people with the intention of trying to destroy them. He explained that the word did not necessarily mean the **mass killing** of all members of a particular group. He wanted a word to describe the way in which different actions are planned and organized with the intention of destroying the identity of a targeted group.

## Tibet

What mattered for Lemkin was the intention, not whether it involved large-scale killing nor whether it was successful or not. The Chinese government has been accused of genocide against the people of Tibet, a **nation** that was forcibly taken over by the Chinese in 1949–50. Tibetans are being taught to think of their nation as a natural part of China. The Dalai Lama, one of their highest religious leaders has been replaced within Tibet by a substitute who accepts Chinese rule. In ways such as this, the ability of Tibetans to think of themselves as an independent people is gradually being destroyed.

## International law

As a result of the **Nazi** government's genocide of Jewish people during **World War II** (1939–45), a legal document called a Convention was agreed on by the **United Nations**. It defined genocide as an international crime, which means it is a crime wherever it happens. A government of one country cannot legalize genocide by making a new law just for itself. The Convention took up Lemkin's idea that genocide is the intention to destroy a group, whether or not large-scale killing takes place.

In recent years, support for the idea of international law has been growing. In 2001, the Prime Minister of Israel, Ariel Sharon, faced charges in a Belgian court over his responsibility for the massacre of Palestinian civilians at the Sabra and Chatila refugee camps in Lebanon in 1982. In 2003, the Belgian government was persuaded by the USA to stop the charges, but the idea of international law has continued to gain strength.

# Genocide on trial

## Nazis on trial

The first people to face charges of genocide were 24 high-ranking **Nazis** and their accomplices who were put on trial at Nuremberg in Germany in 1946. All but three were found guilty because there was plenty of evidence to prove their guilt, and 12 were sentenced to death by hanging. However, the trials have been criticized because the judges all came from the **nations** that had won the war and they were only interested in war crimes committed by the defeated countries. The court did not allow any comparisons to be made with the bombings of German and Japanese cities that had killed so many civilians.

The arrest in 1960 of another Nazi, Adolf Eichmann, led to a more sensational **genocide** trial. This was partly because it was televised and partly because of the dramatic way in which he was captured. Secret agents working for the Israeli government had tracked him down to Argentina, where he was living. He was seized by the agents and brought to Jerusalem to face charges arising from the important part he had played in organizing the genocide of Jewish people. He was tried in 1961 and was found guilty and executed the following year.

Slobodan Milosevic standing trial for genocide at the International Criminal Court in The Hague in 2001.

# United Nations courts

In 1993, the **United Nations** formed the International Criminal **Tribunal** to put on trial people held responsible for genocide in Bosnia and neighbouring countries. In 2001, after a trial lasting over a year, General Krstic, a Bosnian Serb, was found guilty on eight charges, including two of genocide. He was sentenced to 46 years of imprisonment. In 2002, the trial began of Slobodan Milosevic on charges of genocide. He is the first former head of state to be tried on such charges. It is thought that the work of the Tribunal will last until 2010.

The United Nations has also formed a special Tribunal to bring to justice people responsible for the genocide in Rwanda. At the end of 2003 three people, two of whom were journalists (see page 32), were the first to be found guilty and sentenced for this crime. The United Nations has also played an important role in creating a permanent International Criminal Court (see below).

# Case study  The International Criminal Court

In 1998 the United Nations agreed to create a permanent International Criminal Court (ICC), which came into force in 2002. Its task is to investigate and bring to justice people who commit international crimes like genocide and war crimes. By 2004, over 90 countries had signed up to accept the ICC but some countries, including the USA and Israel, were refusing to do so.

# Opposing racism

Racism – thinking people of another race are inferior to your own race – is a common factor in many of the **genocides** that have taken place around the world. Although someone can be a nationalist (believing in the worth of your own country) without being a racist, extreme **nationalism** and racism are often linked. The two beliefs can support each other and help create the kind of hatred for people of a different race which has led in the past to genocide. Governments and their politicians often use racism to gain or increase power and this may also lead to the conditions in which genocide takes place.

In the past, people and governments that thought it was proper to take over land in other countries did so because they believed their race was superior. They often explained or excused what they were doing by saying they were bringing the benefits of their superior race to another country. Nowadays, few countries create colonies in the way they once did, but **imperialism** – the control of a country by another more powerful **nation** – is still a fact in the world and racism still contributes to this.

The good news is that racism is something that people can oppose in their everyday lives. It does not require international courts or the **United Nations** to treat people from different races as equal to yourself. Choosing to behave and think in a non-racist way is something that affects our everyday lives, how we relate to strangers as well as our neighbours.

Sometimes, it is necessary to recognise racism when it is disguised as something else. Newspapers and politicians sometimes broadcast alarming stories about immigrants and refugees and make some people in a country feel that their way of life is under threat. This is what the **Nazis** did, blaming Jews for all sorts of problems in Germany, and people who were taken in by this voted for the Nazi party and helped bring about a genocide. The Nazis admitted they were racists but nowadays groups that are racist are likely to disguise the fact and say they are trying to solve other sorts of problems.

Nazi literature from the 1930s promoted the idea that Germans were a racially pure people – always white, ideally blond-haired and blue-eyed, and never with any suggestion of racial mixing.

WINTER-KAMPFSPIELE
der Hitler Jugend
GARMISCH-PARTENKIRCHEN 23. FEBR. – 2. MÄRZ 1941

# Ethics

'Stop genocide in Chechnya' reads the sign protesting to Vladimir Putin, the Russian President, who was meeting with EU leaders in Europe in 2002.

**Ethics** is a word for describing the rules for acting in ways that are good. Behaving or thinking in a way that is racist, for example, is unethical. **Genocide** is obviously unethical, but just saying this will not stop genocide happening. It is necessary for individuals to act ethically, even though this can be difficult in the kind of circumstances that lead to genocide.

## Innocent bystanders?

Ordinary people may allow themselves to become involved in genocide, often as bystanders who do not interfere to prevent it happening. Or, worse still, they allow themselves to be convinced that some group of people deserve to be punished. Worst of all, they agree to help punish this group and actively take part in what turns out to be a genocide.

authorities refused to **deport** their Jews, and in Bulgaria ordinary people blocked railway lines to prevent Jews being deported. In Denmark, a German official warned the Danish authorities in 1943 that Danish Jews were going to be collected together and deported. The ordinary people of Denmark acted quickly and organized the escape of 6500 Jews, using their own boats to move them at night to safety in Sweden.

**❝The real problem is in the hearts and minds of men. It is not a problem of physics but of ethics.❞**

Albert Einstein, the scientist whose discoveries helped lead to the development of nuclear weapons. From *Becoming Evil*, James Waller.

Ethics is based on the idea that individual people, or a community of people or a whole society, can choose to act in ways that do not harm other groups of people. Society's ethics failed during the **Nazi** genocide and they fail in most cases of genocide. There are, however, examples to show that this need not always be the case. Until the Nazis invaded Italy in 1943, the Italian

## Letting it happen

Genocides happen because most people do not act to prevent them happening. Through fear, prejudice or selfishness – or a combination of these feelings and attitudes – they allow genocide to happen, or take part in it themselves. Acting ethically sometimes requires people to disobey. In situations where hatred against a group is being stirred up by a powerful group or a government, it may well be necessary to disobey authority. In both Nazi Germany and the **USSR** there were many millions of genocide victims and very few people acted to try and prevent it. Both these countries had cultures that taught people to obey authority and not to question it.

# Global ethics

A peacekeeping soldier from the United Nations on duty in West Africa.

The idea of a community, rather than just individuals, acting ethically can also be used when discussing international organizations like the **United Nations** (UN). The UN brings together representatives of all the countries in the world and hopes to prevent the kind of conflicts that may lead to war and **genocide**.

The UN hopes to find a peaceful way of settling a conflict. If a genocide is happening, or about to happen in a country, the UN can agree to send an army to stop the violence and protect the victims. In such cases, the UN would be acting **ethically** on a global, world-wide, scale.

**"It was rather like wanting Hitler to reach a ceasefire with the Jews."**

The UN ambassador of the Czech Republic, angry at the way the UN avoided taking action in Rwanda by merely talking about trying to get a ceasefire. From *A People Betrayed*, L R Melvern.

In the build-up to the genocide in Rwanda, there were UN, French and Belgian soldiers there. When it seemed likely that violence was about to break out, the French and Belgian soldiers were ordered to rescue citizens of their own two countries who were living in Rwanda. They did this, and then left Rwanda. It has been said that if they had remained in Rwanda, the killing could have been stopped.

When the killing started in Rwanda, the UN was warned by people there that genocide was about to take place. The UN, however, was reluctant to take action and found excuses for doing nothing. Powerful member countries of the UN had no interests in Rwanda that they wanted to protect and this made them reluctant to act. One British politician, Tony Worthington, annoyed at the way his country seemed uninterested in what was happening, said that if 'half a million white people had died', instead of black Africans, more attention would have been paid to the problem. The politician felt that race had played a part in delaying governments from acting ethically.

# Hopeful conclusions?

The year after the Rwandan **genocide**, there was another genocide and again countries failed to act **ethically**. Some 30,000 Muslims in Bosnia had fled to the town of Srebrenica in the hope of finding safety from Serb attackers. This time the **UN** did send troops to the town to protect them and declared Srebrenica a 'safe area'. In July 1995, however, Serbs gained control of the surrounding area and attacked the town. No foreign government was willing to take action, and UN troops were ordered to do nothing as Serbs rounded up thousands of refugees. Over the course of a few days, armed Serbians murdered around 7000 unarmed Muslim men and boys and, using bulldozers, buried their victims in mass graves.

Events like those at Srebrenica make it difficult to draw hopeful conclusions about preventing genocide. Most governments, it seems, find it difficult to act ethically when it does not serve their own, more selfish, interests. Those that do try to act ethically are usually in less powerful countries. This is because smaller governments, though as capable as larger ones of acting unethically, tend to be less powerful and do not have selfish interests they want to protect.

## Individual actions

More hopeful conclusions can be drawn from the fact that individual people, acting alone or in groups, have resisted genocide. The examples of Bulgarians, Danes and Italians during the **Holocaust** show how people have not only refused to go along with genocide but were able to act to prevent it. What is also important is the fact that when people resisted **Nazi** persecution of Jews, they had an effect on the behaviour of the

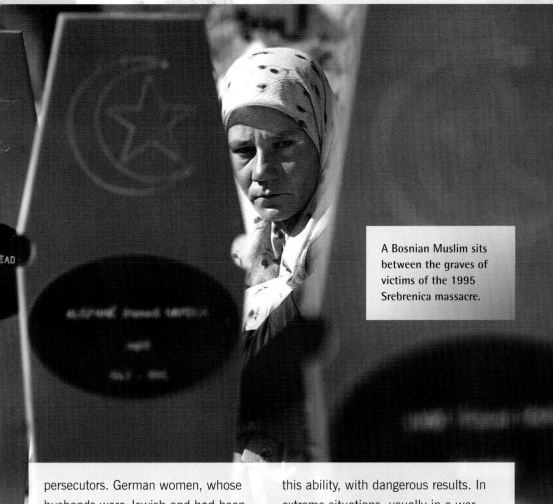

A Bosnian Muslim sits between the graves of victims of the 1995 Srebrenica massacre.

persecutors. German women, whose husbands were Jewish and had been arrested because of this, protested in public outside the prison and demanded their release. Wishing to avoid bad publicity, the authorities released the men and their lives were saved.

The hopeful conclusion is that people can, and usually do, care about other people and try to act kindly. The causes of genocide suggest that conditions sometimes develop where people lose this ability, with dangerous results. In extreme situations, usually in a war, people may want to blame some other group for their unhappiness. If people have been taught to pick on other people's differences, and see themselves as superior, this can lead to genocide. Governments and other countries may not care, and may allow hatred to develop or even encourage it. Ordinary people, acting ethically, can resist this and can hope to prevent the hatred turning into genocide.

**49**

# Facts and figures

## Definition of genocide in international law

From the **United Nations**, *Convention on the Prevention and Punishment of the Crime of Genocide*, 1948:

**Article II**
In the present Convention, genocide means any of the following acts committed with intent to destroy, in whole or part, a national, ethnical, racial or religious group, as such:

(a) Killing members of the group;
(b) Causing serious bodily or mental harm to members of the group;
(c) Deliberately inflicting on the group conditions of life calculated to bring about its physical destruction in whole or part;
(d) Imposing measures intended to prevent births within the group;
(e) Forcibly transferring children of the group to another group.

**Article III**
The following acts shall be punishable:
> Genocide
> Conspiracy to commit genocide
> Direct and public incitement to commit genocide
> **Complicity** in genocide.

Article 6 of the *Rome Statute of the International Criminal Court*, effective from 1 July 2002, defines genocide in exactly the same terms and quotes Article II of the United Nations Convention.

# Major genocides

| Place | Victims | Date | Est. no. killed | Perpetrator |
|---|---|---|---|---|
| Congo (Democratic Republic of Congo) | Congolese | 1885–1908 | unknown millions | King Leopold II and his colonial administration |
| Hereroland (Namibia) | Herero | 1904 | 60,000 | German state |
| Turkey | Armenians | 1915–16 | over 1 million | Ottoman (Turkish) State |
| Ukraine (**USSR**) | Ukrainians | 1932–33 | 4–6 million | Soviet state |
| Nanking (China) | Chinese | 1937 | 260,000 | Japanese state |
| Death camps in Europe | Jews | 1942–45 | 6 million | **Nazi** German state |
| Manila (Philippines) | Filipinos | 1945 | 100,000 | Japanese state |
| Guatemala | Guatemalans | 1960–96 | 200,000 | Guatemalan state |
| Bangladesh | Bangladeshis | 1971 | 1 million | Pakistani state |
| Cambodia | Cambodians, Vietnamese | 1975–79 | 1.5 million | Khmer Rouge state |
| Bosnia | Muslims, Croats, Serbs | 1992–95 | 200,000 | Serbian-Yugoslav state |
| Rwanda | Rwandans | 1994 | 500,000 | Rwandan state |

# Further information

## International contacts

For more information, the following organizations are useful:

**The Aegis Trust**
PO Box 2002
Newark
Nottinghamshire NG22 0PA
UK
Tel: 01623 836978
email: office@aegistrust.org
**www.aegistrust.org**

**Amnesty International**
99–119 Rosebery Avenue
London EC1R 4RE
UK
Tel: 020 7814 6200
Fax: 020 7833 1510
email: info@amnesty.org.uk
**www.amnesty.org.uk**

**Genocide Watch**
PO Box 809
Washington DC 20044
USA
Tel: +1 703-448-0222
email: info@genocidewatch.org
**www.genocidewatch.org**

**Survival International**
6 Charterhouse Buildings
London EC1M 7ET
UK
Tel: 020 7687 8700
email: info@survival-international.org
**www.survival-international.org**

## The Internet

**Prevent Genocide International**
**www.preventgenocide.org**
The website of the Center for the Prevention of Genocide

**www.historyplace.com/worldhistory/genocide**
General information on genocide in the modern world

**The Campaign to End Genocide**
**www.endgenocide.org**
A website promoting a campaign to bring about the end of genocide

**The Armenian National Institute**
**www.armenian-genocide.org/**
A website dedicated to preserving a record of the Armenian genocide

**The Friends of Bosnia**
**www.friendsofbosnia.org**
A website that records the genocide that took place in Bosnia during the 1990s

**www.cybercambodia.com/dachs**
Information on the Cambodian genocide

**The United States Holocaust Memorial Museum**
**www.ushmm.org/**
The official website of the Holocaust Memorial Museum in Washington, DC

**www.hrw.org/reports/1999/rwanda**
Information on genocide in Rwanda

**www.infoukes.com/history/famine**
Information on the genocide in the Ukraine

# Further reading

The Holocaust: Causes, Patricia Levy
(Hodder Wayland, 2001)

The Holocaust: Death Camps, Sean
Sheehan (Hodder Wayland, 2000)

The Holocaust: Life and Death in the
Camps, Jane Shuter (Heinemann
Library, 2002)

The Holocaust: Prelude to the Holocaust,
Jane Shuter (Heinemann Library, 2002)

The Holocaust: The Camp System, Jane
Shuter (Heinemann Library, 2002)

A Little Matter of Genocide: Holocaust and
Denial in the Americas, 1492 to the
Present, Ward Churchill (City Lights Books,
1998)

Talking Points: Genocide, R G Grant
(Hodder Wayland, 1998)

Troubled World: Africa: Postcolonial
Conflict, David Downing, (Heinemann
Library, 2003)

Troubled World: Conflict: India and
Pakistan, David Downing, (Heinemann
Library, 2003)

World Issues: Genocide, Alex Woolf
(Chrysalis Books, 2003)

**Adult reading:**
Becoming Evil, James Waller
(Oxford University Press, 2002)

The Capture and Trial of Adolf Eichmann,
M Pearlman (Weidenfeld and Nicolson,
1963)

Hitler's Willing Executioners: Ordinary
Germans and the Holocaust, Daniel
Goldhagen (Abacus, 1997)

The Holocaust on Trial, D D Gutenplan
(Granta, 2002)

A People Betrayed, L R Melvern
(Zed Books, 2000)

The Pol Pot Regime, Ben Kiernan
(Yale, 2002)

The Rape of Nanking: The Forgotten
Holocaust of World War II, Iris Chang
(Penguin, 1997)

The Roots of Evil, Ervin Staub
(Cambridge University Press, 1989)

# Glossary

**anti-Semitism**
a strong dislike of people because they are Jewish

**Assyria**
an ancient kingdom of the Middle East, most powerful around 800 BCE

**atrocities**
extremely wicked acts, usually involving violence

**bayonet**
a blade attached to the end of a rifle

**biological**
to do with our bodies as a whole, not our minds

**civil war**
war within a country, not against another country

**colonialism**
the policy of a government to form colonies in other countries

**colony**
the settlement formed when a group of people come from outside, usually from another country, to settle and rule a country or part of a country

**communist**
member of a Communist party, believing in an economic system based on state ownership of all means of production and distribution

**complicity**
sharing responsibility for a crime

**concentration camp**
a guarded prison camp in which selected groups of people are confined and, under the Nazis, killed

**Crusades**
the invasions of lands in the Middle East by Christian armies, between 1096 and 1272

**culture**
the customs and beliefs of a people that help give them a sense of identity

**deportation**
removing someone from a country, usually against their will

**eliminate**
to remove, get rid of

**empire**
a group of nations under the authority of one powerful country

**ethics**
a code of behaviour or a set of rules for acting in ways that are good

**ethnic cleansing**
the forced expulsion of one ethnic group by another to create an ethnically pure population

**ethnic group**
a group with a common nationality or culture

**exterminate**
to destroy completely

**gene**
chemical information which determines, for example, the colour of our eyes, that is inherited by children from their parents

**genocide**
the deliberate and organized killing of a group of people, with the intention of destroying their identity as an ethnic, cultural or religious group. The word comes from the ancient Greek word *genos* (race) and the Latin *cide* (killing).

**ghetto**
a restricted area where a minority ethnic group is segregated

**heresy**
an opinion or belief that is not normally accepted

**historical approach**
looking at a situation in terms of what has happened in the past

**Holocaust**
the genocide of over six million Jews, organized by the Nazi government of Germany during World War II (1939–45)

**imperialism**
the act of one country bringing other countries under its authority and creating an empire

**mass killing**
killing people on a large scale

**mass media**
the main means of communication, especially television and newspapers

**Middle East**
the region of the world between Egypt and Iran, including Israel and Iraq

**morale**
the feeling of confidence belonging to a group or an individual

**nation**
a community of people of a mostly common descent, often with its own language

**nationalism**
a strong belief in the value of the nation

**Nazi**
the name of the German government, and its supporters, who carried out the genocide of Jewish people during World War II

**perpetrator**
a person or state held responsible for a crime

**pogrom**
an organized persecution or extermination of an ethnic group. It comes from the Russian word for destruction, after violent mob attacks on Jews in Russia in 1881 and 1903–06.

**political**
to do with relations of power in society, and the ways in which one group of people maintain their power and influence over other groups

**psychological approach**
viewing something in terms of people's state of mind

**scapegoat**
a person or group who is unfairly blamed for something

**sterilized**
no longer able to have children

**traumatic**
something that causes shock

**tribunal**
a court of justice, like the ones organized by the United Nations to investigate the genocides in Rwanda and Bosnia

**United Nations (UN)**
international body set up in 1945 to promote international peace and cooperation

**USSR**
the shortened name for the former Union of Soviet Socialist Republics, dominated by Russia, which broke up at the end of the 1980s

**World War II**
a war between 1939 and 1945 in which Nazi Germany occupied most of Europe, and Japan occupied many parts of Asia. The Allies that defeated Germany and Japan included Britain, the USA, Australia and New Zealand.

# Index

# Titles in the *Just the Facts* series include:

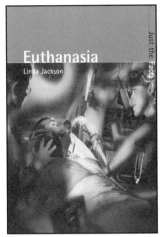

Hardback    0 431 16174 7

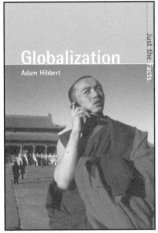

Hardback    0 431 16175 5

Hardback    0 431 16176 3

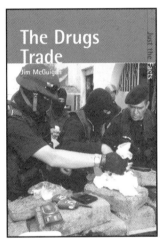

Hardback    0 431 16177 1

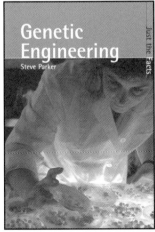

Hardback    0 431 16178 X

Hardback    0 431 16179 8

Find out about the other titles in this series on our website www.heinemann.co.uk/library